AT PASSAGES

BOOKS AND CHAPBOOKS BY MICHAEL PALMER:

*An Alphabet Underground*

*For a Reading*

*Sun*

*Songs for Sarah*

*First Figure*

*Notes for Echo Lake*

*Alogon*

*Transparency of the Mirror*

*Without Music*

*The Circular Gates*

*C's Songs*

*Blake's Newton*

*Plan of the City of O*

# MICHAEL PALMER

## AT PASSAGES

This book is a
gift to the Library
from

E. V. Griffith

A NEW DIRECTIONS BOOK

Manufactured in the United States of America
New Directions Books are printed on acid-free paper
First published as New Directions Paperbook 803 in 1995
Published simultaneously in Canada by Penguin Books Canada Limited

AUTHOR'S NOTE: I am grateful to the editors of the various magazines in which some of these poems first appeared: *American Poetry Review, Avec, Blue Mesa, Colorado Review, Conjuctions, Denver Quarterly, disClosures, Epoch, fragmente, Grand Street, Infolio, Interference, New American Writing, Occident, Sagetrieb, Sakura, Sulfur, Talisman.*

Acknowledgment is made as well to the following anthologies: *The Best American Poetry 1990* (eds. Jorie Graham and David Lehman, Scribners); *The Best American Poetry 1992* (eds. Charles Simic and David Lehman, Scribners); *The Best American Poetry 1993* (eds. Louise Gluck and David Lehman, Scribners); *The New Freedoms: Contemporary Russian and American Poetry* (eds. Edward Foster and Vadim Mesyats, Stevens Institute of Technology); *American Poetry Since 1950. Innovators and Outsiders* (ed. Eliot Weinberger, Marsilio Publishers); *From the Other Side of the Century: a New American Poetry 1960–1990* (ed. Douglas Messerli, Sun & Moon Press); *The Gertrude Stein Awards in Innovative North American Poetry* (ed. Douglas Messerli, Sun & Moon Press); *50: A Celebration of the Sun & Moon Classics* (ed. Douglas Messerli, Sun & Moon Press); *American Poets Say Goodbye to the Twentieth Century* (ed. Andrei Codrescu, Four Walls, Eight Windows); *Exact Change Yearbook No. 1* (ed. Peter Gizzi, Exact Change).

A small selection of these poems was published, with Danish translations by Poul Borum and illustrations by Jens Birkemose, as *An Alphabet Underground* (After Hand, Copenhagen).

I would also like to express my gratitude to the John Simon Guggenheim Foundation and to the Lila Wallace—Reader's Digest Fund for their support at various stages of the writing of this book.

**Library of Congress Cataloging in Publication Data**

Palmer, Michael, 1943–
    At passages / Michael Palmer.
       p.     cm.
    ISBN 0–8112–1294–7 (acid-free paper)
    I.  Title.
    PS3566.A54A92    1995
    811'.54—dc20
                                     94–43613
                                       CIP

New Directions Books are published for James Laughlin
by New Directions Publishing Corporation
80 Eighth Avenue, New York 10011

# Contents

# AT PASSAGES

# LETTERS TO ZANZOTTO

## Letter 1

Wasn't it done then undone, by
us and to us, enveloped, sid-
erated in a starship, listing
with liquids, helpless letters—
what else—pouring from that box,
little gaps, rattles and slants

Like mountains, pretty much worn down
Another sigh of breakage, wintering
lights, towers and a century of hair,
cloth in heaps or mounds, and limbs,
real and artificial, to sift among

Did they really run out of things
or was it only the names for things
in that radial sublimity, that
daubed whiteness, final
cleansing and kindness, perfect
snow or perfection of snow

leaving us peering at the bridge,
its central syllable missing,
and the ground here and there
casually rent, cartoon-like,
lividly living, calling in counter-talk:

*Whoever has not choked on a word*

But Dr. Sleep and his Window of Time?
Pallas and Vesta? Antibodies in plants?
Torches, cobbles and red flags?
The calcined walls facing whenness
meant as witness. The few
trans things smelling of sex and pine

said what to them
and to us as them

## Letter 2

Belowabove: hum of the possible-to-say?

Forest in which the trees grow downward
and through the leaves and mist a small boat in flames?

Song of the closed mouth?
Of an alphabet underground?

## Letter 3

Our errors at zero: milk for mist, grin
for limbs, mouths for names—or else hours

of barks, stammers and vanishings, nods
along a path of dissolving ice. The sign

we make for "same as"
before whatever steps and walls,

shutters flapping in the lighted body
called null or called vocative. I'd wanted to ask

about dews, habits of poplar, carousel,
dreamless wealth, nets, embers

and folds, the sailing ship "Desire"
with its racks and bars

just now setting out. This
question to spell itself. And the waves of us

following what follows,
retelling ourselves

what we say we've said
in this tongue which will pass

## Letter 4

*Almost* or *more than* or *almost alive*

But the body of another you attempt to lift,
the body you try to address
and the doubtful or the dark
of this sudden, stripped
winter and its winds?

A train housed in glass?

And the "supplement of sun"?

But the body you enter
with your tongue, with
the words on its tip,
words for chemicals and tastes
and almost remembered names,

hurriedly chalked equations
for the kinds of snow in our time
and always, behind

the landscape,
a snow more red than white?

## Letter 5

Desired, the snow falls upward,
the perfect future, a text
of wheels. You were born here
between noise and anti-noise
in first bits of film,

silvers of image, the *of*
and its parts—particle
as wave—the perfect
future's steps, its thousand lakes
bells, remarks, lunations and dismays

Days were called the speed book
then the scream book, rail
book then the book of rust, perfect-
bound, perfect shadow of a clock
the photophilographer assembles in negative,

negative sun or negative shade,
negative dust pulled from the ground
and the images negated in ornate frames,
firebricks, funnels and trucks,
figment and testament as one  *

## Letter 6

Dear Z,
So we accused mimesis, accused

anemone
and the plasma of mud,

accused pleasure, sun
and the circle of shadow

## Letter 7

But the buried walls and our mouths of fragments,
*no us but the snow staring at us* . . .

And you Mr. Ground-of-What, Mr. Text, Mr. Is-Was,
can you calculate the ratio between wire and window,

between tone and row, copula and carnival
and can you reassemble light from the future-past

in its parabolic nest
or recite an entire winter's words,

its liberties and pseudo-elegies,
the shell of a street-car in mid-turn

or scattered fires in the great hall
I would say not-I here I'd say *The Book of Knots*

I'd say undertows and currents and waterspouts,
streaks of phosphorous and riverine winds

Dear Z, I'd say it's time, it's nearly time, it's almost, it's
        just about, it's long
past time now time now for the vex- for the vox- for the
        voices of shadows,

time for the prism letters, trinkets and shrouds,
for a whirl in gauzy scarves around the wrecked piazza

Messieurs-Dames, Meine Herren und Damen, our word-balloon,
        you will note, is slowly
rising over the parched city,

its catacombs, hospitals and experimental gardens,
its toll-gates, ghettos and ring-roads,

narcoleptics and therapists and stray cats
Ladies and Gentlemen, our menu for this flight,

due to temporary shortages,
will be alpha-omega soup, Bactrian hump, and nun's farts

As we enter the seventh sphere, you will discover a thin
layer of ice just beginning

to form on your limbs
Do not be alarmed, this is normal

You will experience difficulty breathing, this is normal
The breathing you experience is difficulty, this is normal

Dear Z, Should I say space
constructed of echoes, rifts, mirrors, a strange

year for touring the interior
Should I say *double dance, Horn, axis* and *wheel*

Dear A, Scuttled ships are clogging the harbors
and their cargoes lie rotting on the piers

Prepare executions and transfusions
Put on your latest gear

Letter 8

(cirrostratus)


So *A*'s finally, alephs and arcades,
the bone-dice thrown

beside the chained gates
And the cawing of out-there: bells, charged hearts, old films

threaded past narrative's lip
But what does the whir- the wer- what does the word

need—world need to be gone—to perform—what
does the world

before you need
to become perfect

They are swimming below the cliff-heads and the wind
Brickworld, chimneys, when-if-not-

When-if-not-when, foam
and wrack, wheeling of terns

And aloud, unearthed
as a language of nets

Actual blue and citron
Actual grey underleaf—so

many bundles to burn—take them to the woods
and burn them in heaps

A's before B's
Take the versions in your mouth

Take inside into your mouth
unearthed, all smoke, blue

and citron, actual word
for that earth and that smoke

# SEVEN POEMS
# WITHIN A MATRIX
# FOR WAR

H

We sat on the cliff-head
before twin suns.

For all I know we were singing
"Dancing on the Ceiling."

Descending I became lost
but this is nothing new.

From the screen poured
images toward me.

The images effected a hole
in the approximate center of my body.

I experienced no discomfort
to my somewhat surprise.

This was many weeks ago
many times of days ago.

Yet as far as history goes
it was no time at all.

Many kinds of days ago
I should have said above.

The body has altered
many times since.

Has bent a little over on its stem
and shed a layer of film.

Winter has come and gone
should be remembered.

White occasions like clouds
she may once have whispered.

To that I would add, fields
unplanted, some still burning.

Wonderless things
days at a time.

As a storm begins as a night storm
to end as an ice storm.

Some by now certainly have left
to seek shelter in the mountains.

Only to be met there
by the force of spring rains.

Paths turned to mud
boulders torn loose from above.

The difficulties with burying the dead
she may then have said.

But this letter is something like a door
even if a false door.

Unvoiced as breath
voiced as ash.

To that I would add
there is a song opposite itself.

To that I would add, we have drawn
necessary figures from the sack of runes or tunes.

Echo and wormwood
conspire at the base of the throat.

Snail climbing acanthus
measures our pace.

On the plate by the mark of difference
a mark is made we call the first mark.

Weathering so
the wheel of days.

Gaia the bag lady
in sadness below.

## Construction of the Museum

In the hole we found beside the road
something would eventually go

Names we saw spelled backward there

In the sand we found a tablet

In the hole caused by bombs
which are smart we might find a hand

It is the writing hand
hand which dreams a hole

to the left and the right of each hand

The hand is called day-inside-night
because of the colored fragments which it holds

We never say the word desert
nor does the sand pass through the fingers

of this hand we forget
is ours

We might say, Memory has made its selection,
and think of the body now as an altered body

framed by flaming wells or walls

What a noise the words make
writing themselves

for E.H.
11 apr 91

## Untitled (April '91)


*La narrativa* says you must paint a flower
paint a flower with a death's head

flower with a death's head at its center
center with a desert at its center

clock with ochre hands
its face a sun the sun

a multiple sun at 3 a.m.
sun of limbs and sun of the lens

flower as if it were a limb
anemone, rose, yellow marigold

gravity a word from the narrative
word that bends in the narrative

as if suns would flower as sparks of paint
then fall before the retinal net

fall into actual space
space of minarets and streets

Says, Here is a word you must erase
a word made of particles of paint

Here is a word with no points in space
The Higgins black ink has dried in its bottles

so it's true, as angels have said
that there are things of glass

light-gatherers, cat's-eyes, keys and bells
and that glass is a state of sand

It's impossible to hold such a key in your hand
and it's light you see traveling through angels of glass—

through knells—
causing the il- lis- les- the li- lil- lit-

forming the l's you're never to understand
like the tongues of syllables wreathed in the wells,

like tongue-tied and transparent angels
The painting wall still stands

Studio at night
Everything in place

to P.G.

# H

Yet the after is still a storm
as witness bent shadbush
and cord grass in stillness

sand littered with the smallest of fragments
whether shell or bone
That city we are far from

is still frozen, still in ruins
(except its symmetries be renewed
by sleep, its slant colors redeemed)

Nothing has changed but its name
and the air that it breathes
There's still no truth in making sense

while the ash settles, so fine that
planes keep falling from the sky
And the name once again to be the old one

Saint Something, Saint Gesture, Saint Entirely the Same
as if nothing or no one had been nameless in the interim
or as if *still* could be placed beside *storm*

that simply, as in a poem
Have you heard the angels with sexed tongues,
met the blind boy who could see with his skin,

his body curled inward like a phrase,
like an after in stillness or a letter erased
Have you seen what's written on him

as question to an answer or calendar out of phase
Add up the number of such days
Add *illness* and *lilt* as formed on the tongue

Add that scene identical with its negative,
that sentence which refuses to speak,
present which cannot be found

## Wheel

You can say the broken word but cannot speak
for it, can name a precise and particular shade
of blue if you can remember its name
(Woman of the South, New Lilac, Second Sky?)

As the light, close to blinding, fell—falls
in bars across a particular page, this
then another, some other
followed far too closely by night

Or as the sleeping
pages recall themselves, one by one,
in dream-riddled, guarded tones,
recall themselves from path

to sloped meadow, meadow
to burnt shore, shore
to poised wave, dismay
to present, any present

of the bewildered and the buried alive
(we've been told they were buried alive)
Is there a door he hasn't noticed
and beyond it a letter which created the door

or claims it created a door
which would open either way

## Twenty-four Logics in Memory of Lee Hickman

The bend in the river followed us for days
and above us the sun
doubled and redoubled its claims

Now we are in a house
with forty-four walls
and nothing but doors

Outside the trees, chokecherries, mulberries and oaks
are cracking like limbs
We can do nothing but listen

or so someone claims,
the Ice Man perhaps, all enclosed in ice
though the light has been shortening our days

and coloring nights the yellow of hay,
scarlet of trillium, blue of block ice
Words appear, the texture of ice,

with messages etched on their shells:
*Minna 1892, Big Max and Little Sarah,*
*This hour ago*

*everyone watched as the statues fell*
Enough of such phrases and we'll have a book
Enough of such books

and we'll have mountains of ice
enough to balance our days with nights
enough at last to close our eyes

## "or anything resembling it"

The hills like burnt pages
Where does this door lead

Like burnt pages
Then we fall into something still called the sea

A mirrored door
And the hills covered with burnt pages

With words burned into the pages
The trees like musical instruments attempt to read

Here between idea and object
Otherwise a clear even completely clear winter day

Sometimes the least memorable lines will ring in your ears
The disappearing pages

Our bodies twisted into unnatural shapes
To exact maximum pleasure

From the view of what is in any case long gone and never was
A war might be playing itself out beyond the horizon

An argument over the future-past enacted in the present
Which is an invisible present

Neva streaming by outside the casement
Piazza resculpted with bricolage

Which way will the tanks turn their guns
You ask a woman with whom you hope to make love

In this very apartment
Should time allow

What I would describe as a dark blue dress with silver threads
And an overturned lamp in the form of a swan

A cluster of birches represents negativity
Flakes of ash continue to descend

We offer a city with its name crossed out
To those who say we are burning the pages

# SIX HERMETIC SONGS

for Robert Duncan

*Bring along the Makhent boat*
*for I have come to see Osiris*
*lord of the* ansi *garment*

How did we measure
It says we measured up and down
from the sepia disk
to the crowded ship
of Odysseus

How did we measure
It says we measured
with a copper thread
from the plum flower
to the forgotten gift

Was the tain's smoke
equal to song
the vein of cedar
to a pin's bones
Burns each

earlier day
in its soundless weight
measured by the nets
of air
Go there

You can bring down a house with a sound.
Not to understand this.
But we builded it.

Not with periods (the
sentence) or any sense of design—
sight or sound.

Builded it while blind.
Rain came in.
Noises not ours.

Steps called walls.
Model of a house.
Work we had done before.

In-
harmonics as when
as children

still writing,
writed, written,
interrupted, begun.

The body in fog and the tongue
bracketed in its form

The words as if silvered—coated
and swallowed, cradled and erased

The marks whereby the body
was said to be a world

The walled rehearsals
The curve of abandon,

twinned and masked
The calls and careless fashionings,

digits thrown like dice
I don't think about that anymore

Send me my dictionary
Write how you are

There were nine grand pianos in my father's house
one a water object in my head
and one a ship of glass

one an eye on the end of a branch
and one a paint-pot spilling red
There were live fandangos in the father's house

so that sleepers might sleep within the dance
and set their images to rest
Please tell me if you can

Did it snow pure snow in some father's house
and did the children chant Whether me this
then Whether me that

There was a winding stair in this father's house
climbing or falling no one would say
There were notebooks and nightbooks

and voices enclosed by a ring of bone
They were crying Wait Don't Wait
There were travelers standing at the gate

At the fever of tongues
the metron, with wandering eye

————

At the zero of streets and of windows
an arm in geometry

————

At the circus of nets
at the torn first
edge of an image
the unit of distance
between the eye and the lid

————

At the swarm of the messengers

————

At the storm of fine dust

————

At the pillars and the receiving paths

————

At the hidden roads of the disk

————

At the body of the speaking boat

The wrecked horn of the body
and a water voice

The horn of the body
and a slanted water voice

The notes against the gate
and the erasures at the gate

The mineral swimmers fixed
in a stone's milk

and the doorways of our disappearing
Whose night-songs and bridges

and prisms are these
Whose evens and odds

cats on high limbs
scorpions and swallows

What figures within the coil
tortoise and Bennu bird

lotus and hawk
palette plus ink-pot

# THREE RUSSIAN SONGS

## Who Is To Say

Who is to say
that the House of Tongues is not that place
where rats swarm around your feet
under blooming sofas

is not that place
of poisoned snows, pens run dry
and secrets now too late to know
and certainly the murmuring there below

was a mur- was a mur- was a
murmuring almost to be heard
a bubbling like water
invisible, underneath

And look the shadow of a wing
does fall here as blood
does drink deeply of itself
and does whisper yes for no

Once these faces behind glass
might have returned your glance
might even have gathered up
their limbs, in order to stand

Who is to say
that certain of their words did not spill out
as far as the eyes of cats could see
across the river in the dark

Leningrad
15 sept 90

## Poem

So we traveled
with a mote in each eye

always parallel
to horizon, always sideways

Clouds rose from crumbling brick
where symmetries spoke of bread

They spoke of letters lost
in cellars and halls

and whispered the coming of snow
though far too softly to be heard

## Fontana Dom

Somewhere before the gate
or at the iron gate
or as a kind of gate

Somewhere within the court
the wet loam of the court

As somewhere inside a room
before the photograph of a photograph

Before a braided rope

Dark blue dress with silver threads

Before the mention of birch
cupola, caw of crows
almost sunken boat

Or the circles of ice as they grow
in silence on the windows

# THE LEONARDO
# IMPROVISATIONS

1

Can the
two be

told the
two bodies

be told
apart be

told to
part can

the two
be drawn

the two
be drawn

apart

## 2

What of the words reversed,
words meant

for mirrors, words lost, voices
heard, mirrors

which return. What of the
body there,

the body which turns, the
face which

returns the gaze. What of
the backward

book, the hidden book, the
waves of

bent light in ascending air.
What possible

eye requires such blank signs.
What worlds

appear as more than real
reflected there.

3

First write of all water
in each of its motions

Then eddies of air
in the form of bell towers

Then a book of the building of cities
and the burning of cities,

book of the winged man and the hanged man,
book of miter and argonaut, nautilus,

double helix of the twin stair,
book of the moon as mirror

and words made of mirrors,
book of the body and its memory,

body as a measure and body as a question,
book which explains our shadows,

book of the ram's horn lute and the monochord,
the intervals of light along its string,

book of the trace and book of the fragment,
book of the earth split in half

4

The measure of the actual body
is the measure

of the imaginary body
The body is encircled—

a circle is drawn—
circle that is impossible

around an actual body
body which tastes of salt

and does not exist
within the perfect circle

it fashions around itself
and whose circumference it touches

with the tips of the fingers outstretched
and the soles of the feet at rest

The body is framed by mirrored words
It is not visible in the mirror

The circle and the body meet
on the plane of the imaginary page

5

Curl of leaf and wave
Curve of neck and thigh

As much the unseen
as the visible

As much what has disappeared
as what remains

---

Note: these poems were part of a collaboration with the
Italian painter Sandro Chia. They were first published in a
1991 limited, bilingual edition by Edizioni della Bezuga, in
Florence, under the title, *Improvvisazioni su Leonardo*.

# UNTITLED

# Untitled (February '92)


Sleep said: the unpronounceable shadows
dance and slide and memorize lullabies

Said: a flame is as clear as music
Anything before that is just a fog

a muffled sound between X and now
where swollen bodies have been stacked like logs

as if a lexicon were to swallow its letters
or a swallow devour its young

all the while emitting its click song
which rises and will continue to rise

until it's joined to ink among the gathering clouds
whose scribbled meanings can leave no doubt

Words are made of electrons it turns out
Words remind us of fragments it turns out

parts of legs and parts of arms
It's invisible ink which blots them out

## Eighth Sky

It is scribbled along the body
Impossible even to say a word

An alphabet has been stored beneath the ground
It is a practice alphabet, work of the hand

Yet not, not marks inside a box
For example, this is a mirror box

Spinoza designed such a box
and called it the Eighth Sky

called it the Nevercadabra House
as a joke

Yet not, not so much a joke
not Notes for Electronic Harp

on a day free of sounds
(but I meant to write "clouds")

At night these same boulevards fill with snow
Lancers and dancers pass a poisoned syringe,

as you wrote, writing of death in the snow,
Patroclus and a Pharaoh on Rue Ravignan

It is scribbled across each body
Impossible even to name a word

Look, you would say, how the sky falls
at first gently, then not at all

Two chemicals within the firefly are the cause,
twin ships, twin nemeses

preparing to metamorphose
into an alphabet in stone


St.-Benoît-sur-Loire
to Max Jacob

## SB

So a seed or syllable pitched into the well
disturbs the cloud-form, tears

the image from the bone. And so our weathers
ink themselves together,

dorsal crests and billows missewn
for a cloak. And you say,

Gaze of a breeze, empty sleeve.
You say, It has begun, has started

to begin, a little like mist.
And Mr. Dust (Street of Bees) insists

that there were hours, apples and stones,
terms of a circle marking what?

And coins grown dark, dogs
and cats against the factory walls,

tiny islands of gelatin light,
a dim go and all gone,

our thens to void the sunken head,
hands and the voiceless rest,

equal plod equal ground,
measured step by step.

# Recursus

The voice, because of its austerity, will often cause dust to rise.

The voice, because of its austerity, will sometimes attempt the representation of dust.

Someone will say, I can't breathe—as if choking on dust.

The voice ages with the body.

It will say, I was shaped by light escaping from a keyhole.

Or, I am the shape of that light.

It will say, For the body to breathe, a layer must be peeled away.

It will say, What follows is a picture of how things are for me now.

It will say, The rose is red, twice two is four—as if another were present.

The dust rises in spirals.

It will say, The distance from Cairo to anywhere is not that great.

As if one had altered the adjustment of a microscope.

Or examined its working parts.

Possibly an instrument covered with dust and forgotten on a shelf.

Beside a hatbox and a pair of weathered boots.

The voice will expand to fill a given space.

As if to say, This space is not immeasurable.

This space is not immeasurable.

When held before your eyes.

And which voice is it says (or claims to say), Last night I dreamt of walls and courses of brick, last night I dreamt of limbs.

As you dream—always unwillingly—of a writing not visible and voices muffled by walls.

As if the question: lovers, prisoners, visitors.

The voice, as an act of discipline or play, will imitate other voices.

This is what I am doing now.

This is what I'm doing now.

The clock behind my back, its Fusée mechanism.

Voice one recognizes from years before.

Beneath water, hidden by a spark.

Here at the heart of winter, or let's say spring.

Voice with a history before its eyes.

With a blue dot before its eyes.

History of dust before its eyes.

It will say, as if remembering, The letter S stands for a slow match burning.

On the table before me.

No numbers on this watch.

And I live in a red house that once was brown.

A paper house, sort of falling down.

Such is the history of this house.

It looks like this.

Looks just like this.

We think to say in some language.

to Porta

## Erolog

(a reply)


Asked, Don't you dream, do you ever
or once, did you once—the white

(he)—the white
rain, railings, head-high, erased, no

shadow. And our menhirs, watch-
towers, carbon shores, our almosts—

of speaking, or speaking-seeing, her
lifting, the alphabets and nets.

And the body—listen—and the
body—who's to say—tossed up

in storm the night before.
Or the gnomon or the hourglass or a comb

drawn slowly through the hair
again and again, the droplets of sweat

intermingling, each one a lens, each a question
visible along the surface of the skin.

But did you ever—do you—did you once—
or then—did you then—nights

(he)—nights
had their sentries and gates,

passages where—decibels—maybe folds where—
and I'm speaking from memory here,

memory could not interfere.
So if the fingers, lunate,

could remember the hand
could account for it

could summon the wrist,
fashion gestures and figures.

And if the hallways and stairs,
the slow flares as they settled

to perplex geometry,
angels invisible at the parapets

and the bent, lettristic acrobats
now deaf, held still and

fearing themselves. And you think
you are making a picture

uttering a sound
saying a thing

and you pretend to wrest the helix from its sleep,
to free its threads

amidst the rubble of the square,
whoever was awake and waiting there.

We pointed toward space
as it is before day.

## In C

Pared and lettered to an edge
of X, figured forward

toward a shore—who
would look, who call

a canceled glance from a throat
All calm blocks rehearse loss

All flex spends notes
light as a thought, all

starred, all crossed
Will our poor wrecks sink gleaming ships,

erase each
pure built image

Will our stabs meet ends,
our nils a century's redress

# Disclosures

## 1

Beneath the writing on the wall
is the writing it was designed

to obscure. The two together
form a third kind

## 2

There is no writing
on the wall's other side

Perhaps this lack
constitutes a fourth kind

## 3

Some of the writing on the wall
will be designated as truth

some as art

## 4

It is said to represent a mirror
of everyday life in its time

## 5

"Fabius Naso
talks through his asshole

and shits out his mouth"
for example


6

"Foute les Arabes"
for example


7

Certain words and images
or parts of images

have been chipped away
These often turn up for sale

at sidewalk stalls
before the walls

of other cities


8

I too have an image for sale
It's the image of a poem

and is to be found
on the reverse of this sheet

## Untitled (Far Away Near)

Still early still late
Have we asked enough questions about space
and what surrounds space
and the hands of a body tumbling through space

Still early still late
as a leaf might curl in a certain way
thinking to turn into carbonized lace
and a body might hurtle through space

Does a color experience pain
while falling through endless space
falling like a blob of sun or a peacock's call
(This June we have no rain at all)

How far away are the voices you hear
and those you can't seem to recall
Does each color recite a name
as if it were its own

yet almost unknowable like a fragrance of plums
(Your house is under repair your house is gone)
Question of the signs the bodies before us form
illegible as dust or eye of noon

Why did the Angel Phosphor arrive
in that city on that (white) night
caduceus held forward in its hand
We had joked that there was no city only winter

no winter only wind
only early and lateness, only streets and blown pages
then the day's final words
traced in silver fluid at the edge of the stage

What then if we spelled "after" with different letters
the letters for "first" or "last," for example
for "forest of burning boats" or "farther"
and it came to mean "the chaos of the waterwheel"

or "the glow of the Thomson lamp"
What if spoken in muteness or danced without memory
What if as elsewhere or blinded, but watching the fire
helix of flames in the center of a square

Have we asked enough questions about changes of light
over time
Use music if you want
Yet let it not reach the ear


                                              for the dancers

## Untitled

O you in that little bark
What is the relation of the painting to its title

The painting bears no relation to its title
The tiny boat bears

nameless people across
water that is infinitely dark

darker even than snow on paving stones
darker than faces in shadow on a boat

The boat is called Blunder, or Nothing, or Parallel Lines
The poem was called I Forget, then Empire, then Game of Cards

a game played yesterday in milky light
light which played across the players' faces

and the arcane faces of the cards
There is no relation between the painting and its title

The painting came first then its title
The players are playing cards in a little boat

They are asleep and it is dark
Their dream is called The Orderly Electrons

One traveler dreams she does not belong
Another dreams with his eyes wide open

like a solemn philosopher
dead from an act of thought

Two more lie with limbs intertwined
The painting has no title

though it has been signed Keeper of the Book
the signature obviously forged

for D.S.

## Red Yellow Blue

(Sarah's Eighth)


Now that you know all the words
and I have almost forgotten them

Or now that you have experienced rain
for days on end

and learned to paint with red, yellow and blue
those days which seem to have no end

and I see you often walking alone
down the street or else among friends

mindful of company, equally wondering
wherefrom a world's wrongs stem

And now that you may swim out of sight
if you choose, as choose you must

all along,
a song

## Writer's Dream (Untitled)

Untitled
and at night
a pen identical
with all other pens

and untitled at night
a "dream within a movie
called *The Petrified City*"
wherein you pictured

mistakenly
more light
Later it would be called
"Writer's Dream"

because it had no words
only certain
distances to serve
in place of a title

## An Anniversary

What was it
that code of cloud
a wave and then
a sudden expelling
rattle of final breath
across our path

What was it
we saw
were meant to see
scattered bones rusting cups
heaved up
in dark of sun

How was it formed
this sea of ash and lime
and intermittent light
How would we read
its instructions
How proceed

Doubtless by now I owe you some nickels
for this mildewed book
decades overdue
I hardly even began it
since it seemed built of a grammar
whose laws were secret

## Writer's Dream (The Wagon)

Out of the city's
early morning mist
a horse-drawn wagon

piled high with limbs
Said the white-bearded carter:
*In winter a coal wagon*

*but in summer ice*
*Today I'm hauling*
*a full load of gifts*

*It was the Angel of Syntax*
*who commanded this*

*commanded this of me*
*for spring*

for I.P.

## Untitled (September '92)


Or maybe this
is the sacred, the vaulted and arched, the
nameless, many-gated
zero where children

where invisible children
where the cries
of invisible children rise
between the Cimetière M

and the Peep Show Sex Paradise
Gate of Sound and Gate of Sand—
Choirs or Mirrors—
Choir like a bundle of tongues

Mirror like a ribbon of tongues
(such that images will remain
once the objects are gone)
Gate of the Body and Gate of the Law

Gate of Public Words, or Passages,
of Suddenness and Cells, Compelling Logic, Gate
of the Hat Filled with Honey
and Coins Bathed in Honey

As the light erases
As heat will etch a d, a design, a
descant of broken lines into glass
Exactly here

between thought and extended arm,
between the gate named for lies
and the double X of the empty sign,
a kind of serous field,

fluid scene or site
peopled with shadows
pissing blood in doorways
yet versed in the mathematics of curves,

theory of colors,
history of time
At Passages we peer out
over a tracery of bridges,

patchwork of sails
At Desire is it possible
we speak without tongues
or see only with tongues

And at Lateness we say
*This will be the last*
*letter you'll receive,*
*final word you'll hear*

*from me for now*
Is it that a fire
once thought long extinguished
continues to burn

deep within the ground,
a fire finally acknowledged
as impossible to put out,
and that plumes of flames and smoke

will surface at random
enlacing the perfect symmetries
of the Museum of the People
and the Palace of the Book

Or that a Gate of Hours speaks
in a language unfamiliar,
unlike any known,
yet one clear enough

clear as any other
and clear as the liquid
reflection of a gate,
gate whose burnt pages

are blowing through the street
past houses of blue paper
built over fault lines
as if by intent

## Untitled (kN)

We made a week of eight days
Each day a new bird spoke

from a bird book, a book of streets and names
codices and vanishings

Each new day we passed the body's name
from hand to hand, eye to ear

according to a script spoken by the ear
on the second day, maybe the third

incomprehensible to us all
in sleep, this promise

or week of promises
and parallel songs

Press your hands everywhere said the songs
to each other back and forth

there's a book infinite as scissors
there's an irreparable book

a fragment like an arm
Let's make a week of eight days

each one the last to itself
each a book uttering a phrase

and each the remnant of one page
from a bird book, a forgotten book

of intervals, a lost book
Run your fingers down the page

## Untitled (March '93)

As what's-his-name says in 109, movement three
I went to that favorite magazine store
to find an image
but it was closed

permanently closed it seems
by means of an ancient lock and key,
went to her ear for a word or more
The inclination of her head

beneath the rain instructed me
As David said in a recent letter
the time's about to arrive for someone close
someone I almost know

the false sky has never been this blue
and by blue I mean a specific blue
made of letters I forget—
call it this or that

The train departs during such a period
in such weather: storm from the northwest
lasting as long as a single night
which can't be divided

The two embracing in the courtyard below
must know that even the stars' bond betrays
Still let's happily believe in the figure
for a while. It's enough

## From the Anthology (W's Dream)

A book full of dark pictures
or was it a poem
discovered in a book
whose first line read

"A book full of dark pictures"
dark as the river of Eros
or Creation's mists
Who will even notice

among such images
if we should exchange breath
for breath, enter
each other

with pain and pleasure mixed
as in a book full of dark pictures
dark as a dream of translation
or Creation's mists

## Under the Perseids

Even as it passes
we can't make out its name

Yet a river of stone
could have been a river

and the b—the buzz—of blessing
might have been all knowledge

swimming in a blank book
a stone book opened flat

or maybe just a phrase book
where bread translates as bread

felt opposite of itself
and a listing boat—a stone boat—

mistakes its tongue for a sail
An encounter, it says

as if such were as simple
as tossing dust in the air

There is a list, it says, more or less
of what we are, what we own

a window and a door
the steps leading in

These glasses are mine, for example,
this question, the angle of a gaze

the paradise it describes
and the one it denies

A few friends are seated on a verandah
in impossibly heavy air

The music floating up
seems some combination

of theramin and washboard
fiddle and mandolin

We do not believe it
Do we believe instead

in the blue of history,
the flare of a spirit lamp

bridging two bodies,
how the surface of the hand

will imitate a map
Whatever it is

*mirror to mirror*
that suddenness of crows

tremor as the body opens
always perishing

to Jerry Estrin

## Far Away Near

"We link too many things together"
                              Agnès Rouzier

As it's said in The Fragments
I met the blind typist

inventor of words
The iris of the eye

is an inverted flower
and the essay on snow

offers no beginning
only an aspect of light

beneath a gate
only a photograph of earth

only a fold
a grammar reciting its laws

Just as the clatter
seems distant

and dies without further thought
that moment we ask

*Have we reached the center yet,* or
*Should there be more blue do you think*

*or just a different shade of blue*
all the while tacitly acknowledging

that by blue
she might have meant red

and by red . . .
As it's said

we must train our guns toward the future
where the essay on light will obviate time

and the essay on smoke
will cause the ground to open

One day I completed the final word
of a letter to my father

in what key I forget
After the ink had dried

I noticed the rain lit by a streetlamp
shaped like a conical hat

I noticed the map
of the moon you had left

half in shadow on my desk
In a city near the North Sea

white nights passed as I read
of an aviator downed

in the Barr Adjam
during the war directly after

the war to end all wars
sightless and burned across

three-fourths of his body
Listening in twin silences

his name had disappeared
from his lips

As it's said in The Fragments
There once was a language with two words

and the picture of an apple tree
As it's said

The ravens present a paradox
We learn a new gesture

utter unintelligible sounds
in a cheerful voice perhaps

pointing to the sky
where the rain continues

# Autobiography

All clocks are clouds.

Parts are greater than the whole.

A philosopher is starving in a rooming house, while it rains outside.

He regards the self as just another sign.

Winter roses are invisible.

Late ice sometimes sings.


*A* and *Not-A* are the same.

My dog does not know me.

Violins, like dreams, are suspect.

I come from Kolophon, or perhaps some small island.

The strait has frozen, and people are walking—a few skating—across it.

On the crescent beach, a drowned deer.


A woman with one hand, her thighs around your neck.

The world is all that is displaced.

Apples in a stall at the streetcorner by the Bahnhof, pale yellow to blackish red.

Memory does not speak.

Shortness of breath, accompained by tinnitus.

The poet's stutter and the philosopher's.

The self is assigned to others.

A room from which, at all times, the moon remains visible.

Leningrad cafe: a man missing the left side of his face.

Disappearance of the sun from the sky above Odessa.

True description of that sun.

A philosopher lies in a doorway, discussing the theory of colors

with himself

the theory of self with himself, the concept of number, eternal return, the
sidereal pulse

logic of types, Buridan sentences, the *lekton*.

Why now that smoke off the lake?

Word and thing are the same.

Many times white ravens have I seen.

That all planes are infinite, by extension.

She asks, Is there a map of these gates?

She asks, Is this the one called Passages, or is it that one to the west?

Thus released, the dark angels converse with the angels of light.

They are not angels.

Something else.

for Poul Borum

## Small Night Song for Jacques Roubaud

In the night of glass
we hear certain songs

*and certain things*
*sharp and simple*

*commonplace*
*take on a face*

*figured as cypress*
*figured as shade*

*And my eyes*
*And my eyes*

Glass of night
Glass of night

# Autobiography 2 (hellogoodby)

The Book of Company which
I put down and can't pick up

The Trans-Siberian disappearing,
the Blue Train and the Shadow Train

Her body with ridges like my skull
Two children are running through the Lion Cemetery

Five travelers are crossing the Lion Bridge
A philosopher in a doorway insists

that there are no images
He whispers instead: Possible Worlds

The Mind-Body Problem
The Tale of the Color Harpsichord

Skeleton of the World's Oldest Horse
The ring of O dwindles

sizzling round the hole until gone
False spring is laughing at the snow

and just beyond each window
immense pines weighted with snow

A philosopher spread-eagled in the snow
holds out his Third Meditation

like a necrotic star. He whispers:
archery is everywhere in decline,

photography the first perversion of our time
Reach to the milky bottom of this pond

to know the feel of bone,
a knuckle from your grandfather's thumb,

the maternal clavicle, the familiar
arch of a brother's brow

He was your twin, no doubt,
forger of the unicursal maze

My dearest Tania, When I get a good position in the courtyard
I study their faces through the haze

Dear Tania, Don't be annoyed,
please, at these digressions

They are soldering the generals
back onto their pedestals

for A.C.

# CITES

---

"The sun beat down through a sky
that had never seen clouds."
*Chaos*, James Gleick


\*\*\*

"the mark multiplied"

\*\*\*

for Micaëla Henich

can lie, but

under the grey

a part seen

is spherical, is

unearthed, all smoke

an unbridgeable gulf

arched and taut

preceded this gazing

anemone and the

but the buried

strands, salty to

harbors and their

space constructed of

and the cawing

wrack, wheeling of

rising over the

in its parabolic

walls and our

as if in

if no such

and aloud, returning

actual blue and

meant as witness

but the body

all smoke, blue

just so far

severed, its neck

because a focus

plaits, calcined walls

seems to be

or alternate flooding

rushes were once

absence of certain

or cling there

but another part

our distance to

patterns he can

as a net

dark, swallowing itself

of grey, spun

without legs or

shadows appear to

one sheltered against

smoked mirrors which

an hypothesis and

bits of bone

from ferrous mud

the mark multiplied

hull, hollow but

sea always seemed

to count them

buried there had

centuries, although they

thicker making it

fanned or flayed

les pierrailles les

against the fallen

as if blood

retreat into their

were to knot

where it falls

du large qui

spiral of dark

is subject to

sea to intermittent

remains attached to

an etching on

from a vortex

perspective of duration

where it spills

to penetrate between

slow and measured

est creusé dans

at intervals as

to read the

levels to extreme

through its ribs

so shapes its

neither our nor

will die if

glasswort or samphire

where the black

with perfect blades

the direction they

at each margin

cycle, the missing

when their plumes

the most, inscribed

page of a

and who before

a desire no

outcome of differences

their boundaries which

flicker over it

but the sudden

two-note calls are

as if bodies

channels that they

as when ash

que mes yeux

where clear green

mineral crust had

the mouths of

waiting to be

displacement by degrees

and rill marks

discover a thin

assembles in negative

dust pulled from

citron, actual word

tongue which will

of this sudden

its world, before

arrival of a

so shapes its

twin in its

bare line of

from the crest

an E or

the spine of

there (as Daive

the peat that

and the dispersal

registered as time

an X set

nothing but ink's

or beyond it

called the whorl

single or in

dark as our

to gravity so

can still see

and position for

may retain much

where no oxygen

wash ashore after

and almost iridescent

quickens and subsides

if the possible

wherever such tremors

then resurface as

sheered at an

as if signs

seen from above

and without thought

carries an atmosphere

where shore encircled

an equilibrium determined

to flood the

body, threads of

into its forked

surely it never

read as traces

since the wind

the water boatmen

so wantonly along

sun without its

dark twin to

imagine a red

the sphere forms

there in fragments

or a mill?

where tides often

so elder, groundsel

(a spell of

or itself surrounded

messages children had

color (for instance)

or else imagined?

what the names

one speaks one

different when I

windrow of rock

the sign R

(found only where

is not seen

that a word

is always supposed

to be possible

but can we

not sometimes speak

of a darkening

not sometimes feel

like saying if

we were without

memory we would

find ourselves there

mantled by a

violent night sky

above those same

cliffs, ochre and

silver, scored with

jagged rivulets, remnants

of a stair

or slatted fence

and beyond, rutted

walkways by walls

the door's A

prolapsed in shadow

a raised arm

Note: "Cites" represents my text for a multiple collaboration undertaken by the visual artist Micaëla Henich, who lives in Paris. Other writers participating were Jacques Derrida, Dominique Fourcade, Tom Raworth and Jacques Roubaud. "Cites" is to be published in a limited edition by Théatre Typographique, Courbevoie, France, with two hundred *encre de Chine* drawings by the artist.